The POWER OF DISCIPLINE

7 WAYS IT CAN CHANGE YOUR LIFE

BRIAN TRACY

Table of Contents

Introduction 5

Self Discipline and Goals 8

Self Discipline and Character 26

Self Discipline and Time Management 40

Self Discipline and Personal Health 50

Self Discipline and Money...............................64

Self Discipline and Courage.............................76

Self Discipline and Responsibility...................92

The POWER OF DISCIPLINE

"Discipline is the soul of an army.
It makes small numbers formidable,
procures success to the weak,
and esteem to all."

GEORGE WASHINGTON

INTRODUCTION
By Brian Tracy

Why are some people more successful than others? Why do some people make more money, live happier lives and accomplish much more in the same number of years than the great majority?

I started out in life with few advantages. I did not graduate from high school. I worked at menial jobs. I had limited education, limited skills and a limited future.

And then I began asking, "Why are some people more successful than others?" This question changed my life.

Over the years, I have read thousands of books and articles on the subjects of success and achievement. It seems that the reasons for these accomplishments have been discussed and written about for more than two thousand years, in every conceivable way. One quality that most philosophers, teachers and experts agree on is the importance of self-discipline. As Al Tomsik summarized it years ago, "Success is tons of discipline."

Some years ago, I attended a conference in Washington. It was the lunch break and I was eating at a nearby food fair. The area was crowded as I sat down at the last open table by myself, even though it was a table for four.

A few minutes later, an older gentleman and a younger woman who was his assistant, came along carrying trays of food, obviously looking for a place to sit.

With plenty of room at my table, I immediately arose and invited the older gentleman to join me. He was hesitant, but I insisted. Finally, thanking me as he sat down, we began to chat over lunch.

It turned out that his name was Kop Kopmeyer. As it happened, I immediately knew who he was. He was a legend in the field of success and achievement. Kop Kopmeyer had written four large books, each of which contained 250 success principles that he had derived from more than fifty years of research and study. I had read all four books from cover to cover, more than once.

After we had chatted for awhile, I asked him the question many people in this situation would ask, "Of all the one thousand success principles you have discovered, which do you think is the most important?"

He smiled at me with a twinkle in his eye, as if he had been asked this question many times, and replied without hesitating, **"The most important success principle of all was stated by Thomas Huxley many years ago. He said, 'Do what you should do, when you should do it, whether you feel like it or not.'"**

He went on to say, **"There are 999 other success principles that I have found in my reading and experience, but without self-discipline, none of them work."**

Self-discipline is the key to personal greatness. It is the magic quality that opens all doors for you, and makes everything else possible. With self-discipline, the average person can rise as far and as fast as his talents and intelligence can take him. But without self-discipline, a person with every blessing of background, education and opportunity will seldom rise above mediocrity.

In the pages ahead I will describe seven areas of your life where the practice of self-discipline will be key to your success. It is my hope you will find a few "nuggets" that will help make your dreams come true.

All the Best,

Brian Tracy

Chapter 1

SELF-DISCIPLINE &

Goals

"Discipline is the bridge between goals and accomplishment."

JIM ROHN

Your ability to discipline yourself to set clear goals, and then to work toward them everyday, will do more to guarantee your success than any other single factor.

You've heard it said that, "You can't hit a target you can't see."

"If you don't know where you're going, any road will get you there."

Wayne Gretzky said, "You miss every shot you don't take."

It seems that only 3% of adults have written goals and plans, and they earn more than the other 97% put together.
Why is this? The simplest answer is that, if you have a clear goal and a plan to achieve it, your focus is fixed on a set course of action. Instead of becoming sidetracked by distractions and diversions, your time is focused on a straight line from start to finish. This is why people with goals accomplish so much more than people without them.
The tragedy is that everyone thinks they already have goals. But what they really have are hopes and wishes.
A wish has been defined as a "goal with no energy behind it." Hope is not a strategy.

Goals that are not written down and developed into plans are like bullets without powder in the cartridge. People with unwritten goals go through life shooting blanks. Because they think they already have goals, they never engage in the hard, disciplined effort of goal setting, the master skill of success.

USA Today reported on a study a couple of years ago. First, researchers selected people who made New Year's resolutions. Then they divided these people into two categories: those who made New Year's resolutions and wrote them down, and those who made New Year's resolutions, but neglected to write them down.

Twelve months later, they followed up on the respondents in this study. What they found was astonishing! Of the people who made New Year's resolutions but neglected to write them down, only 4% actually followed through on their resolutions.

However, among the group that took a few minutes to record their New Year's resolutions, 44% followed through on them. This difference of more than 1100% proves the simple act of crystallizing resolutions or goals on paper increases likelihood of success.

In my experience of working with several million people over the past twenty-five years, the disciplined act of setting goals, making plans for their accomplishments, and then working on them daily, increases the likelihood of achieving your goals by ten times, or 1000%.

This does not mean that goal setting guarantees success, only that it increases the probabilities of success by ten times. These are very good odds to have working in your favor.

Sometimes I tell my seminar audiences,

"Only three percent of adults have written goals, and everyone else works for them."

Your brain has both a success mechanism and a failure mechanism. The failure mechanism is the temptation to follow the undisciplined path of least resistance, to do what is fun and easy rather than what is hard and necessary. Your failure mechanism triggers automatically throughout your life, which is the major reason why most people fail to fulfill their individual potentials.

A client of mine recently told me an interesting story. He attended one of my seminars in 1995, when I spoke about the importance of writing down your goals and making plans for their accomplishment. At that time, he was thirty-five years old, selling cars for a dealership in

Nashville and earning about $50,000 a year.

He told me that that day changed his life. He began writing out his goals and plans and working on them daily. Twelve years later he was earning more than one million dollars a year and was the president of a fast growing company selling services to the Fortune 500, some of the biggest companies in the world. He told me that he could not imagine what his life would have been like if he had not written down the goals he wanted to achieve in the years ahead.

While your failure mechanism goes off automatically, your success mechanism is triggered by a goal.

When you decide upon a goal, you override your failure mechanism and change the direction of your life.

You go from being a ship without a rudder, drifting with the tide, to becoming a ship with a rudder, a compass and a clear destination, sailing straight toward your destination.

In nature, the homing pigeon is a remarkable bird. It has an uncanny instinct that enables it to fly back to its home roost, no matter how far away it starts or in what direction it must go.

When you decide upon a goal,
you override your failure mechanism
and change the direction
of your life.

Goals

You can take a homing pigeon out of its roost, put it in a cage, put the cage in a box, cover the box with a blanket and put the covered box in the back of a pickup truck. Then drive one thousand miles in any direction, stop the truck, take out the box, remove the blanket, open the cage and throw the homing pigeon into the air.

The homing pigeon will circle three times and then fly straight back to its home roost. This is the only creature on earth, other than human beings, that has this ability.

You also have this remarkable homing ability within your own brain, but with one special difference. The homing pigeon seems to know instinctively exactly where its home roost is located. It then has the ability to fly directly back to that roost.

But human beings, once they have programmed a goal into their cybernetic goal-seeking mechanism, can then set out without having any idea where or how the goal can be achieved. And by some miracle, they will fly unerringly toward the achievement of that goal.

Many people are hesitant to set goals. They say, "I want to be financially independent but I have no idea how I'm going to get there."

As a result, they don't even set it as a goal. But the good news is that you don't need to know how to get there. You just need to be clear about where you want to end up, and your cybernetic goal-striving mechanism in your brain will guide you unerringly to your destination.

THE SEVEN-STEP FORMULA

There are seven simple steps you can follow to set and achieve goals. There are more complex and detailed goal-achieving methodologies, but the Seven Step Method will enable you to accomplish ten times more than you have ever accomplished before, and far faster than you can imagine.

First, decide exactly what you want. Be specific. If you want to increase your income, decide upon a specific amount of money rather than just "make more money."

Second, write it down. A goal that is not in writing is like smoke; it drifts away and disappears. It is unsubstantial and useless. It has no force, effect or power. But a written goal becomes something that you can touch, read and modify if necessary.

Third, set a deadline for your goal. Pick a reasonable time period and write down the rate at which you want to achieve it. If it is a big goal, set a final deadline and then set sub-deadlines or interim steps between where you are today and where you want to be in the future.

A deadline serves as a "forcing system." Just as you often get more done when you are under the pressure of a specific deadline, your subconscious mind works faster and more efficiently when you have decided that you want to achieve a goal by a specific time.

The rule is: "There are no unrealistic goals; there are only unrealistic deadlines."

What do you do if you don't achieve your goal by your deadline? Simple. You set another deadline. A deadline is a "guestimate." Sometimes you will achieve your goal before the deadline, sometimes on the deadline, and sometimes after the deadline.

When you set your goal, it will be within the context of a certain set of external circumstances. But these circumstances may change, causing your deadline to change as well.

Fourth, make a list of everything you can think of that you could possibly do to achieve your goal. **Henry Ford said, "The biggest goal**

can be accomplished if you break it down into enough small steps."

Make a list of the obstacles and difficulties you will have to overcome, both external and internal, to achieve your goal.

Make a list of the additional knowledge and skills you will require to achieve your goal.

Make a list of the people whose cooperation and support you will require to achieve your goal.

Make a list of everything you can think of that you will have to do, and then add to this list as new tasks and responsibilities occur. Keep writing until your list is complete.

Napoleon Hill once said, "The most common reason that people fail to achieve their goals is because they do not make new plans to replace the old ones when the situation changes."

Fifth, organize the list by both sequence and priority.

A list of activities organized by sequence requires that you determine what you need to do first, what you need to do second, and what you need to do later on.

A list organized by priority enables you to determine what is more important and what is less important.

Sometimes sequence and priority are the same, but often they are

not. For example, if you want to start a particular kind of business, the first item in order of sequence might be purchasing a book or enrolling in a course on that type of business.

But what is most important is your ability to develop a business plan based on complete market research. This will provide the information needed to gather the appropriate resources to launch the business.

Sixth, take action on your plan immediately. The difference between winners and losers in life is simply that winners take the first step. They are action-oriented. They're willing to take action with no guarantee of success. They're willing to face failure and disappointment. But they're always willing to take action.

Seventh, do something every day that moves you in the direction of your major goal. This is the key behavior that will guarantee your success. Seven days a week, 365 days a year, do something, do anything that moves you at least one step closer to the goal that is most important to you at the time.

When you do something every day toward the direction of your

goal, you develop momentum. This momentum, this sense of forward motion, motivates you, inspires you and energizes you. As you gain momentum, it is easier to take even more steps toward your goal. In no time at all, you will have developed the discipline of setting and achieving your goals. It soon becomes easy and automatic. You develop the habit and the discipline of working towards your goals all the time.

TEN GOAL EXERCISES

Take out a clean sheet of paper. At the top of the page write the word, "Goals" and today's date.

Then, discipline yourself to write down ten goals you'd like to accomplish in the next twelve months. Write down financial goals, family goals, fitness goals

Goals

1
2
3
4
5
6
7
8
9
10

and personal possessions, like a house or a car.

Don't worry for the moment about how you are going to achieve these goals. Just write them down as quickly as you can. You can write as many as fifteen goals if you like, but this exercise requires that you write down a minimum of ten goals within three to five minutes.

Once you have written out your ten goals, imagine for a moment that you can achieve all of these goals if you pursue them diligently. But also imagine that you have a "magic wand" you can wave that will enable you to achieve any one goal on your list within twenty-four hours.

If you could achieve any one goal in your life within twenty-four hours, which goal would have the greatest positive impact on your life right now? Which one goal would change or improve your life more than anything else? Which one goal, if you were to achieve it, would help you to achieve more of your goals than anything else?

Whatever your answer is to these questions, put a circle around this goal and then write it at the top of a clean sheet of paper. This goal becomes your "Major Definite Purpose." It becomes your focal point and the organizing principle of your future activities.

*If you could achieve
any one goal in your life
within twenty-four hours,
which goal would have
the greatest impact
on your life?*

Once you have written out this goal in clearly defined and measurable steps, set a deadline for your goal. Your subconscious mind needs a deadline so it can focus and concentrate all your mental abilities on goal attainment.

Make a list of everything you can think of doing to achieve your goal. Organize this list by sequence and priority.

Resolve to work on this goal every day until it is achieved. From this moment forward, as far as you are concerned, "Failure is not an option." Once you have decided that this one goal has the potential to have the greatest positive impact on your life, and you have designated it as your major definite purpose, resolve that you will work on this goal as hard as you can, as long as you can, and that you will never give up until it is achieved. This decision alone can change your life.

MIND STORMING

Take another clean sheet of paper. Write out your Major Definite Purpose at the top of the page in the form of a question. Then discipline yourself to write a minimum of twenty answers to the question.

For example, if your goal is to earn a certain amount of money by a certain date, you would write the questions as, "How can I earn $XXX by this specific date?"

Now discipline yourself to generate twenty answers to your question. This exercise of "mind storming" will activate your mind, unleash your creativity and give you ideas that you may never have thought of before.

The first three to five answers will be easy. The next five answers will be more difficult, but the last ten answers will be the most challenging you can imagine, at least the first time you do this exercise. But you must exert your discipline and willpower to persist until you have written down at least twenty answers.

Once you have twenty answers, look over your list and select one of those answers to take action on immediately. It seems that when you take action on a single idea from your list, it triggers more ideas and motivates you to take action on even more of these ideas.

The best application of the law of cause and effect is that "Thoughts are causes, and conditions are effects."

Your thoughts create the conditions of your life. When you change your thinking, you change your life. Your outer world becomes a mirror image reflection of your inner world.

Perhaps the greatest discovery in the history of thought is that,

"You become what you think about most of the time." **The teacher John Boyle said, "Whatever you can think about on a continuing basis, you can have."**

When you think about your goal continually and work on it everyday, your mental resources will be concentrated on moving you toward your goal and moving your goal toward you.

The discipline of daily goal setting will make you a powerful, purposeful and irresistible person. You will develop self-esteem, self-confidence and self-respect. As you feel yourself consistently moving toward your goals, you will ultimately become unstoppable.

"Give me a stock clerk with a goal
and I'll give you a man who will make history.
Give me a man with no goals and
I'll give you a stock clerk."

– J. C. PENNEY

Napoleon Hill the writer said,

Whatever the mind of man can conceive and believe, it can achieve.

Chapter 2

SELF-DISCIPLINE &

Character

"Hold yourself responsible for a higher standard than anyone else expects of you. Never excuse yourself. Never pity yourself. Be a hard master to yourself and be lenient to everyone else."

HENRY WARD BEECHER

The development of character is the great business of life. Your ability to develop a reputation as a person of character and of honor, is the highest achievement of social life.

Ralph Waldo Emerson wrote, "What you do speaks so loud I cannot hear what you say."

The person you are today, your innermost character, is the sum total of all your choices and decisions in life to date. Each time you consistently make good choices and decisions, your character is strengthened and self-worth increases. Conversely, each time you compromise your value system by consciously choosing poor choices, your character is weakened.

A person of character possesses a series of virtues or values. These are courage, compassion, generosity, temperance, persistence, and friendliness, among others. But the most important value in determining the depth and strength of your character is integrity.

It is integrity, living in complete truth with yourself and others, that most demonstrates the quality of your character.

In a way, integrity is actually the value that guarantees all other values. The higher your level of integrity, the more honest you are with yourself, the more likely it is you will live consistently with all other values you admire and respect.

It takes tremendous self-discipline to become a person of character. It takes considerable willpower to always "do the right thing" in every situation. It takes self-discipline and willpower to resist the temptation to cut corners, to take the easy way, or to act for short-term advantage.

All of life is a test, ultimately proving our character. Wisdom can be developed privately, through study and reflection. But character can only be developed in the give and take of daily life, when forced to choose and decide among alternatives.

It is only when you are under pressure, when forced to choose one way or another, that your true character is demonstrated.

Emerson also said,
"Guard your integrity as a sacred thing; nothing at last is sacred except the integrity of your own soul."

You are a "choosing organism." You are constantly making choices, one way or the other. **Every choice you make is a statement about your true values and priorities.** You always choose what is more important, or of higher value to you, over what is less important, or has lesser value, at that moment.

The only bulwark against temptation, the path of least resistance and the expediency factor, is character. The only way to "develop more surely toward the stars" is to exert your willpower in every situation when you are tempted to do what is easy rather than what is correct.

The payoff for becoming a person of character is tremendous. **It demands consistent willpower and discipline to make the right choice when faced with the option of taking the easy way out. The end result is a sense of increased self-worth and self-esteem.**

In addition to feeling positive about yourself when you behave with character, you earn the respect and esteem of people around you. They look up to you and admire you. Doors are opened and new opportunities are presented. You will be paid more and promoted faster, and given even greater responsibilities. As you become a person of honor, all things become possible for you.

You learn values in one of four ways: instruction, study, practice or choice.

One of the chief roles of parenting is to teach your children values. This requires patient instruction with repeated explanations as they grow up. Once is never enough. The value, and the importance of living by that value, must be explained. Instruction includes positive role modeling of the desired value, for example truth, in the face of consequences.

Children are very impressionable to lessons they learn from important people in their lives as they grow up. They accept what their parents say as a fact, as absolute truth. They absorb what is said like a sponge. Like wet clay, you write your description of values on their souls, which becomes a permanent part of the way they see and relate to life.

More than anything else, you demonstrate values in your behavior. Children observe and strive to emulate the values you teach, preach and practice. And they are always watching.

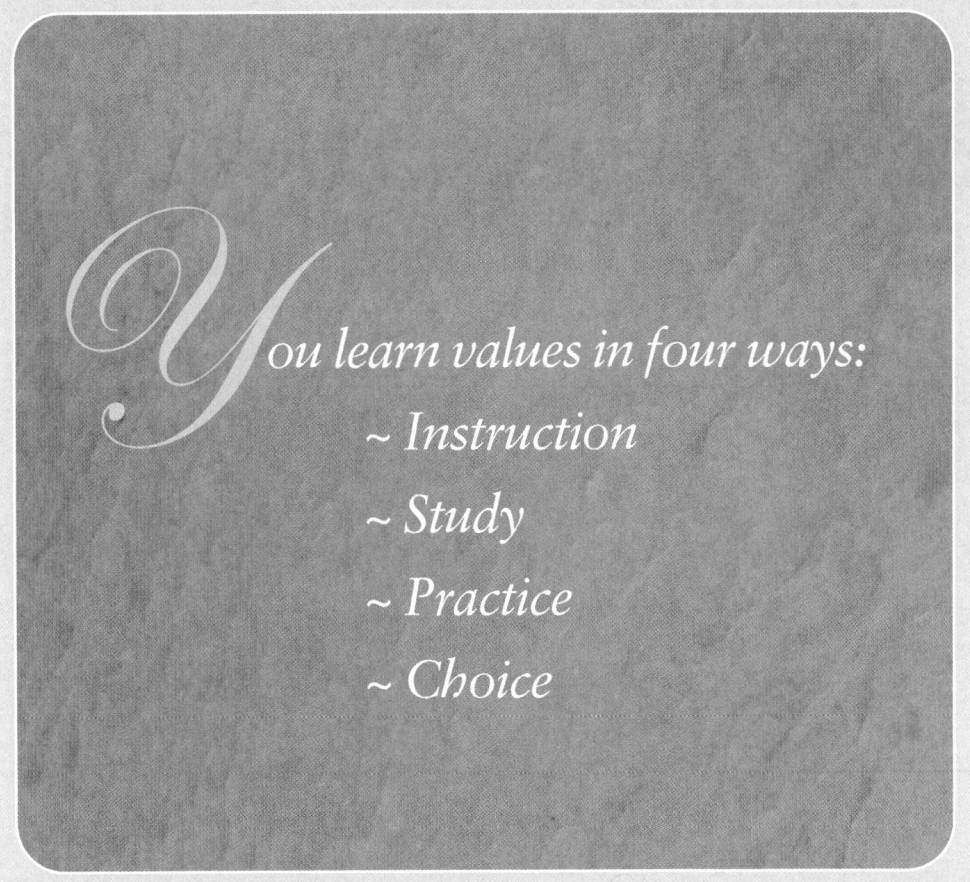

You learn values in four ways:
~ Instruction
~ Study
~ Practice
~ Choice

You learn values by studying them. The Law of Concentration says that, "Whatever you dwell upon, grows and increases in your life."

This means, when you study and read stories about men and women who demonstrate the kind of values you admire and respect, those values become part of your thought process. Once these values are "programmed" into your subconscious mind, they create a propensity within you to behave accordingly when the situation arises.

In military training, soldiers are continually told stories of courage, obedience, discipline and the importance of supporting their fellow soldiers. The more they hear these stories, discuss them, and think about them, the more likely they are to behave consistently with these values when they are under the pressure of actual combat.

Truth defines the core value or virtue of character. Whenever you tell the truth, however inconvenient it may be at the time, you feel better about yourself and you earn the respect of the people around you. One of the highest accolades you can pay to another person is to say, "He or she always tells the truth."

Values are developed by practicing them as situations arise.

As Epictetus said, "Circumstances do not make the man; they merely reveal him to himself." When a problem occurs, you tend to react automatically based on the highest values developed at that moment.

Finally, values are developed by repetition, behaving consistently in a manner until it becomes automatic, and thus a habit. Men and women with highly developed characters behave consistently irregardless of their situation. No question remains about whether or not they did the right thing.

The psychology of character involves the three parts of your personality: your self-ideal, your self-image, and your self-esteem. Your self-ideal is that part of your mind composed of your values, virtues, ideals, goals, and aspirations.

Your self-ideal is composed of those values that you most admire in others and most aspire to possess in yourself.

The most important part of your self-ideal is summarized in the word "clarity." Superior people are those who are absolutely clear

about who they are and what they believe. They have complete clarity about the values they believe in and what they stand for. They are neither confused nor indecisive. They are firm and resolute when it comes to any decision involving values.

On the other hand, weak and irresolute people are fuzzy and unclear about their values. They only have a vague notion of what is right or wrong in any situation. As a result, they take the path of least resistance and act impulsively. They do whatever seems to be the fastest and easiest thing to get what they want in the short term, giving little consideration or concern to the consequences of their acts.

Just as you can classify life forms from least complex to most complex, from a single-celled plankton to a human being, human beings can be classified along a spectrum as well. The lowest forms of human beings are those with no values, no virtues and no character. They always act impulsively and take the path of least resistance in search of immediate gratification.

The highest levels of human development include those men and women of complete integrity, those who would never compromise their honesty or character for anything, including the threat of loss, pain or even death.

The second part of your personality is your self-image. This is the way you see and think about yourself, especially prior to any event of importance. Outward behavior tends to be consistent with self-image. This is often called your "inner mirror" into which you peer before you engage in any behavior.

When you see yourself as calm, positive, truthful and possessed of high character, you behave with greater strength. Other people respect you more. You feel in control of yourself and the situation.

Here is the good news. When you behave in a manner consistent with your highest values, your self-image improves. You see and think about yourself in a better light. You feel happier and more confident. Your behavior and outward performance then reflects this inner picture you have of yourself.

People accept you based on your own self-evaluation. If you view yourself as person of high character, you will treat other people with courtesy, grace and respect. They in turn will treat you as a person of honor and character.

The third part of your personality is your self-esteem. This is how you feel about yourself, your emotional core. Self-esteem is defined as "how much you like yourself."

The more you see yourself as a valuable and important person, the more positive and optimistic you will be. When you consider yourself to be important, you will treat other people as if they are important as well.

Much of your character is determined by the people you most admire, living and deceased. Who are they? Review your life and make a list of the ten people you most admire, and next to their names, write out the virtues or values they most represent.

If you could spend an afternoon with anyone, living or deceased, who would you choose? Why would you choose that person? What would you talk about during your afternoon together? What questions would you ask, or what would you want to learn?

Your role models have a tremendous impact on shaping your character. The more you admire a person and his or her qualities, the more you strive, consciously and unconsciously, to become like that person. This is why clarity is so important.

Whenever you act consistently with your values, you feel good about yourself. Whenever you compromise your values, for any reason, you feel bad about yourself. When you compromise your values, your self-confidence and self-esteem decrease. You feel uneasy and inferior. You feel inadequate and uncomfortable. When you compromise your values, you feel something is fundamentally wrong.

In the development of character, based on self-discipline and willpower, long-term thinking is essential. The more you think about the long term consequences of your behavior, the more likely it is that you will do the right thing in the short-term. When you have to make a choice or decision, ask the magic question, "What's important here?"

Practice the Universal Maxim of Immanuel Kant,

"Resolve to behave as though your every act were to become universal law for everyone."

One of the great questions for the development of character is this, **"What kind of a world would this world be if everyone in it was just like me?"**

Whenever you slip, and do or say something that is inconsistent with your highest values, immediately "get back on your horse." Say to yourself, "This is not like me!" and resolve that next time, you will do better.

The Law of Concentration states, whatever you dwell upon grows and increases in your life. When you think and talk about the virtues and values you most admire and respect, you program them internally into your subconscious until they begin to operate automatically in every situation.

When you live your life consistently, exercising self-discipline and willpower, you move rapidly along the path to becoming a person of excellence.

There is a story told by an old Indian:

On my shoulders are two wolves. One is a black wolf, evil, who continually tempts me to do and say the wrong things. On the other shoulder is a white wolf that continually encourages me to live up to my very best."

A listener asked the old man, "Which of these wolves has the greatest power over you?"

The old Indian replied, "The one I feed."

Chapter 3

SELF-DISCIPLINE &

Time Management

"If you do not conquer self,
you will be conquered by self."

NAPOLEON HILL

There is perhaps no area of your life where self-discipline is more important than in the way you manage your time. **Time management is a core discipline that largely determines the quality of your life.**

Peter Drucker says, "You cannot manage time; you can only manage yourself."

Time management is really life management, personal management, management of yourself, rather than of time or circumstances.
Time is perishable; it cannot be saved. Time is irreplaceable; nothing else can replace it. Time is irretrievable; once it is gone or wasted, you can never get it back. Finally, time is indispensable, especially for accomplishment of any kind. All achievement, all results, all success requires time.
The fact is that you cannot save time; you can only spend it differently. You can only move your time usage from areas of low value to areas of high value. Herein lies the key to success, and the requirement for self-discipline:

Time management is the ability to choose
the sequence of events.

By exerting your self-discipline with regard to time, you can choose what to do first, what to do second, and what not to do at all. And you are always free to choose.

Tremendous self-discipline is required to overcome procrastination that holds most people back from great success. It is said that "procrastination is the thief of life." A native Indian once told me that it is even worse. He said, "Procrastination is the thief of dreams."

The Pareto Principle, the 80/20 rule, says that 20% of the things you do contain 80% of the value of what you accomplish. This means that 80% of what you do is worth 20% or less of the value of what you accomplish.

Because of this disparity, some things you do are five times, and even ten times, more valuable than other things. The challenge for most people is that the most important things you do are big, unpleasant and difficult. The 80% of things you do that make little or no difference to your life are fun, easy and enjoyable.

You can tell the value that something has to you by the amount of time you invest in it.

You always pay attention to and spend time on what you most value, whether it is your family, your health, your social or sports activities or your money and career. **It is only by looking at how you spend your time that you, and everyone else, knows what is really important to you.**

The essence of time management requires you to discipline yourself to set clear priorities, and then to stick to those priorities. You must consciously and deliberately select the most valuable and important thing you could be doing at any given time, and then discipline yourself to work solely on that task.

In your personal life, your goal is to get the highest "return on energy" from your activities. Ken Blanchard refers to this as getting the highest "return on life."

Just as you would be careful about investing your money to ensure the highest rate of return, you must be equally as careful when you invest your time. You must be sure to earn the highest level of results, rewards and satisfaction from the limited amount of time you have.

Always ask yourself before committing to a time consuming activity, "Is this the best use of my time?"

Lack of self-discipline in time management leads people to procrastinate continually on their top tasks, leading them to spend more time

on tasks of low-value or no-value. And whatever you do repeatedly eventually becomes a habit.

Many people have developed the habit of procrastination, of putting off their major tasks. Instead they spend most of their time on activities that make very little difference in the long run.

One of the most important words in developing the discipline of time management is "consequences." Something is important to the degree that it has serious potential consequences for completion or non-completion. A task or activity is unimportant to the degree that it does not matter if it is done or not.

Completing a course of study at the university can have enormous consequences that can impact your life for many years to come. Completing a major task at work, or making an important sale, can have significant consequences on your job and your income.

On the other hand, drinking coffee, chatting with co-workers, reading the newspaper, surfing the Internet or checking emails may be enjoyable, but these activities have few or no consequences. Whether you do them or not makes little or no difference to your work or your life. And it is precisely these activities that most people spend their time on.

There is a simple time management system that you can use to overcome procrastination. It requires self-discipline, will power and personal organization. By using this system, you can double and triple your productivity, performance and output.

Start by making a list of everything you have to do each day. The best time to make this list is the evening before, at the end of the workday, so that your subconscious mind can work on your list of activities while you sleep. You will often wake up with ideas and insights on how to more effectively complete the tasks of the day.

Apply the A B C D E Method to your list:

A = "MUST DO" – Serious consequences for non-completion;

B = "SHOULD DO" – Mild consequences for doing or not doing;

C = "NICE TO DO" – No consequences whether you do it or not;

D = "DELEGATE" – Everything you possibly can to free up more time for those things that only you can do;

E = "ELIMINATE" – Discontinue all tasks and activities that are no longer essential to your work and to achieving your goals.

Review your list of activities for the coming day and write an "A,B,C,D, or E" before each task.

If you have several "A" tasks, separate them by writing A-1, A-2, A-3, and so on. Do this with your B and C tasks as well. The rule is that you should never do a B task when you have an A task left undone. You should never do a lower value task when you have a higher value task before you.

Once you have organized your list using this system, discipline yourself to start on your A-1 task first thing in the morning, before you do anything else.

Once you have begun work on your most important task, you must discipline yourself to concentrate single-mindedly, with 100% of your time and attention, until that task is complete.

It takes tremendous self-discipline to select your most important task, and start on that task rather than doing anything else. But once you begin work on it, you will start to feel a flow of energy that motivates and propels to action. You will feel more positive and confident. You will feel excited and happy. The very act of starting on an important task raises your self-esteem and motivates you to continue.

*Deep within each person
is an intense desire to feel strong,
effective, powerful and in control
of his or her life.
You automatically trigger these feelings
of self-confidence and self-esteem
when you start to work on the task
that is most important to you
at the moment.*

This **ABCDE Method** seldom takes more than ten minutes to organize your entire day. But you will save ten minutes in execution for every minute you invest in this way of planning before you begin.

As you feel yourself moving forward, making progress on your most important task, your brain will release a steady flow of endorphins, nature's "happy drug." These endorphins will make you feel positive, focused, alert, aware and completely in control.

When you discipline yourself to continue to push through against your natural resistance and complete a major task, you achieve an "endorphin rush." You experience this as a sense of elation, exhilaration, happiness and higher self-esteem. By completing a major task, you feel exactly like an athlete who has crossed the finish line first. You feel like a winner.

Your payoff from excellent time management is continuous. As soon as you begin to plan and organize your time, set priorities, and begin on your A-1 task, you will feel happier and more in control of yourself and your life.

Starting today, you should apply these key time management principles to every area of your life. Apply them to your work, your family, your health, your exercise routine and your financial decisions and activities.

You require tremendous discipline to set priorities and then to stick to those priorities. You require the continuous exertion of discipline and willpower to overcome the procrastination that holds most people back.

The more you discipline yourself
to use your time well,
the happier you will feel and the better will be
the quality of your life in every area.

Chapter 4

SELF-DISCIPLINE &

Personal Health

"Self respect is the root of discipline;
the sense of dignity grows with
the ability to say no to oneself."

ABRAHAM JOSHUA HESCHEL

More people are living longer and living better today than ever before in human history, and your goal should be to be one of them. There is no area where self-discipline is more important than in your practices regarding your health. Your number one goal for yourself should be to live as long and as well as you possibly can. This requires lifelong self-discipline regarding your health habits.

The average life expectancy for males today (2007) is 76.8 years; for females 79.8 years, or approximately 80 years, which is increasing each year.

This means that 50% of the population will die below the age of 80 and 50% will die above the age of eighty. Your goal should be to defy the averages and live to 90, 95 or even longer.

The Alameda Study, a study that tracked thousands of people for more than twenty years, concluded there were seven key health habits that contributed the most to long life:

EAT REGULARLY, rather than fasting, starving, or gorging. Eat normal, healthy meals, preferably five or six times per day with your last meal fully three hours before you go to sleep.

EAT LIGHTLY: Overeating makes you tired and sluggish while eating lightly makes you feel healthy and alert.

No snacking between meals: When you eat, your body has to break down and digest the foods in your stomach so they can move into your small intestine and begin the digestive process. This requires four to five hours. If you consume more food on top of food you have already eaten, the digestive process must start over again, with food at several different stages of digestion. This leads to upset stomach, heartburn, drowsiness in the afternoon and constipation.

EXERCISE REGULARLY, about thirty minutes a day, by walking, running, swimming and generally moving your entire body.

WEAR SEATBELTS. Under age 35, the most common cause of premature death is traffic accidents.

NO SMOKING. Smoking is correlated with thirty two different illnesses including lung cancer, esophageal cancer, throat cancer, stomach cancer, heart disease and a variety of other ailments.

MODERATE TO NO ALCOHOL CONSUMPTION. Studies show that one to two glasses of wine per day aid digestion and seem to be beneficial to your overall health. Anything in excess of that can lead to all kinds of problems, including overeating, traffic accidents, personality problems and antisocial behavior.

Each of these seven factors that contribute to long life is completely a matter of self-discipline. They are a matter of choice. They are actions that you can choose to take or not take deliberately. They are completely under your control.

In my personal development seminars, we teach the five "P's" of excellent health:

1. PROPER WEIGHT: This requires a regular exercise of discipline and willpower to achieve your proper weight and then to keep it throughout your life, but the payoff is tremendous. You look good, feel good, and generally feel more positive and in control of your life.

2. PROPER DIET: As Benjamin Franklin said, "Eat to live, rather than

live to eat." According to studies of Olympic athletes from more than 120 countries, the three factors their diets have in common are a lean source protein, a wide variety of fruits and vegetables, and lots of water, about eight glasses per day. When you begin an "Olympic diet," you will feel more alert, awake and focused all day long.

3. PROPER EXERCISE: The most important exercise for long life is aerobic exercise. This requires that you get your heart rate up to a high level for thirty to sixty minutes three times per week. You can achieve this through brisk walking, running, cycling, swimming or cross-country skiing.

Exercise physiologists have determined that the "exercise effect" clicks in after about 25 minutes of vigorous exercise. At this point, your brain releases endorphins which give you a feeling of elation, commonly referred to as a "runners high." This natural drug, produced by your body, can become addictive in a very positive way.

People who develop the habit of regular, vigorous exercise, find that it becomes easier and easier to do. They begin to look forward to the feeling of happiness they enjoy as the result of exercising aerobically.

4. PROPER REST: This is very important. More than 60% of adults do not get enough sleep. They are suffering from what is called "sleep deficit." They go to bed a little too late, arise a little too early, and go through the day in a form of a "fog." This phenomenon, of not being sufficiently rested, leads to poor performance, increased mistakes, industrial accidents, car crashes, short tempers, personality problems, and many other difficulties.

If you are living and working a normal life, you require about eight hours of sleep each night. If you only get six or seven hours of sleep instead of eight hours, you begin to build up this sleep deficit. By the end of the week, when you get up in the morning, the first thing you think of is how soon you can go back to sleep. When you start thinking about sleeping the moment you arise, you know that you are not getting enough sleep.

In addition to eight hours of sleep per night, you need regular breaks from work, including weekends and vacations. When you take time off from work, you allow your mental and emotional batteries to recharge. After a two or three-day weekend, when you go back to work, you will be fully rested and ready to perform at your best.

*Personal
Health*

5. PROPER ATTITUDE: This is perhaps the most important of all. The quality that is most predictive of health, happiness and long life, is "optimism." The more optimistic you are about yourself and your life, the better your health is in every area.

People who are positive and optimistic usually have strong immune systems, and as a result, they are seldom sick. They rarely get colds or flu's. They bounce back quickly from hard work or fatigue. An optimistic person has a built-in "Teflon shield" against many of the diseases and ailments that affect the average person.

The biggest single self-discipline problem people have today is overeating and becoming overweight. More than 50% of Americans are officially overweight, and more than 20% are obese, defined as being more than 30% above their normal weight. There is no area where self-discipline is more necessary than in getting your weight under control, and then keeping it under control for the rest of your life.

You have heard it said that, "Diets don't work." What this really means is that when you starve yourself to lose weight, there is a tendency to put the weight back on almost as quickly as it was lost. There are many reasons for this.

The biggest single self-discipline problem people have today is overeating and becoming overweight. More than 50% of Americans are officially overweight, and more than 20% are obese, defined as being more than 30% above their normal weight. There is no area where self-discipline is more necessary than in getting your weight under control, and then keeping it under control for the rest of your life.

Each person has a certain metabolism. This is the rate at which you burn energy. This metabolic rate is set over the course of your lifetime by the amount of food eaten relative to the amount of exercise expended to work it off.

In addition to your metabolic rate, you have what is called a "set point." This is where your weight is set, and to which it returns, no matter how much you take off as the result of crash dieting. **To lose weight permanently, you must change your set point to a lower number.**

The way you do this is by creating a clear mental image of how you will look when you are at your ideal weight. You then begin a gradual process of changing the quality and quantity of what you eat permanently, with no intention of ever going back.

Many people diet and lose weight with the idea that, as soon as they have dropped a certain number of pounds, they can reward themselves by going out and having a fabulous meal, or consuming unlimited desserts. In other words, they use the idea of filling up on foods as the reward for losing weight. This approach is doomed to fail.

The key to perfect health can be summarized in five words: "Eat less and exercise more."

The only way you can lose weight permanently is to burn off more calories than you consume. There is no other way. And this can only be accomplished over an extended period of time, especially if you have allowed yourself to put on a lot of excess weight.

In my program, "Thinking Big," we teach the importance of avoiding the three white poisons: sugar, salt and flour.

To lose weight permanently and enjoy high levels of health and energy, you should eliminate all simple sugars from your diet. Simple sugars are contained in candy, cake, pastries, soft drinks, canned fruits, sugar in your coffee and all other forms of sugar consumed in large quantities every day. The fact is you require no excess sugar to enjoy superb levels of physical health. By simply eliminating all sugar and sugar products from your life, by going "cold turkey" from sugar, you will begin to lose as much as one pound per day.

In addition, you should eliminate all salt from your diet. The average American gets sufficient salt in all the different foods he eats. But the average American consumes an extra twenty pounds of salt by eating foods with high-salt content, and by adding additional salt to meals.

Personal Health

When you consume excess salt, your body retains water in order to hold that salt in suspension. When you stop consuming excess salt, and simultaneously drink eight glasses of water per day, your body releases all the excess fluid and you actually experience a weight drop as much as four or five pounds in the first day.

Finally, eliminate all white flour products from your diet. This includes all breads, all pastries, all pastas, rice, buns, rolls and anything else made with white flour.

White flour is actually an "inert substance" from which all nutrients have been removed and then bleached out. When you see the words "enriched white bread," they mean that the white flour, which is essentially a dead food material, has been laced with artificial, chemical vitamins, almost all of which have been destroyed in the baking process. There is no food value in a white flour product.

Your goal in life should be to enjoy the highest levels of health and energy possible.

This requires that you eat the right foods and fewer of them. It requires that you get regular exercise and move every joint of your body daily. To enjoy superb physical health, you must get lots of rest and recreation. **Above all, you must maintain a positive mental attitude, looking for the good in every situation, and remain determined to be a completely positive person.**

In each of these areas, the exertion of self-discipline and willpower will give you payoffs that are far beyond the effort you put out. By practicing self-discipline in your health habits, you can live longer and live better than you ever imagined possible.

"*As I see it every day*
you do one of two things:
build health or produce disease
in yourself."

– ADELLE DAVIS

*The key to perfect health
can be summarized in five words:*

*"Eat less and
exercise more."*

Chapter 5

SELF-DISCIPLINE &

Money

"In reading the lives of great men, I found that
the first victory they won was over themselves...
self-discipline with all of them came first."

HARRY S. TRUMAN

According to insurance industry statistics, of one hundred people who start work at age 21, by age 65, one will be rich, four will be financially independent, fifteen will have some money put aside, and the other eighty will still be working, broke, dependent upon pensions or dead.

The primary reason for financial problems in life is lack of self-discipline, self-mastery, and self-control. It is the inability to delay short term gratification. It is the tendency of people to spend everything they earn and a little more besides, usually supplemented by loans and credit card debt.

The good news is that we are living in the best time of all human history. There are more opportunities to achieve wealth and affluence today for more people, in more different ways, than have ever existed in the history of man. It has never been more possible to achieve financial independence than it is today. But you must make a resolution to do it, and then follow through on your resolution.

The primary reason that most adults have financial problems is not because of high expenses. The book, *The Millionaire Next Door,* by Tom Stanley and William Danko, shows how two families living on the same street, in the same size house, and working at the same job, can have completely different financial situations. By the age of 45 or 50, the

couple in one house is financially independent, while the couple next door is deeply in debt and having trouble making the minimum payments on their credit cards.

The reason is not the amount of money they earn. The reason is lack of self-discipline and the inability to delay gratification. Why is this weakness of character so prevalent amongst the majority of adults in today's society? It goes back to early childhood.

When a child receives his allowance or money from a relative, the first thing he wants to do is spend that money on candy. Candy is sweet. Candy is delicious. Candy fills your mouth with a wonderful, sugary flavor. Children like candy and can seldom get enough of it. Many children will eat candy until they become physically ill because it tastes so good.

As you grow older, you develop what psychologists call a "conditioned response" to receiving money from any source. Like Pavlov's dog, when you receive money, you mentally salivate at the thought of spending this money on something sweet and delicious.

When you go on vacation to a resort of any kind, there are hotels and streets lined with shops selling useless trinkets, bobbles and trash, clothes, artwork, and other items you would never think of buying at home. Why is this? Simple. When you are on vacation, you feel happy.

You have a conditioned response to associate happiness with spending money. The happier you are, the more unconsciously compelled you are to go out and spend money on something or anything.

It is quite common for people to go shopping when they are un-happy or frustrated for any reason. They unconsciously associate buying something with being happy. When it doesn't work as they expected, they buy something else. They buy many things they don't particularly need because they unconsciously associate spending with happiness.

As an adult, whenever you receive your paycheck, a bonus, a com-mission, an IRS refund, a prize, or an inheritance, the first thing you do is think about how you can spend this money as quickly as possible.

> **The starting point for achieving financial independence is to discipline yourself to *rewire* your attitude towards money. You reach into your subconscious mind and disconnect the wire between "spending" and "happiness." You then reconnect that "happiness" wire to the "saving and investing" wire.**

From that moment on, instead of saying, "I enjoy spending money," say, "I enjoy saving money."

To reinforce this shift in thinking, open up a "financial freedom account" at your local bank. This is the account in which you deposit money for the long term. Once your money goes into this account, resolve that you will never spend it on anything except to achieve financial freedom.

If you want to save money to buy a boat or a car, open up a separate account for that purpose. But your financial freedom account is inviolable. Never touch it except to invest those funds so that they yield a higher rate of return.

When you do begin saving in this way, something miraculous happens within you. You start to feel happy about the idea of having money in the bank. Even if you only open your account with ten dollars, you gain a feeling of self-confidence and personal power. You feel happy about yourself. The very act of disciplining yourself to save money makes you feel stronger and more in control of your destiny.

And here is something that is absolutely amazing! The Law of Accumulation states "every great achievement is an accumulation of many small achievements." When this is combined with the Law of Attraction, which states "you attract into your life those things that are in

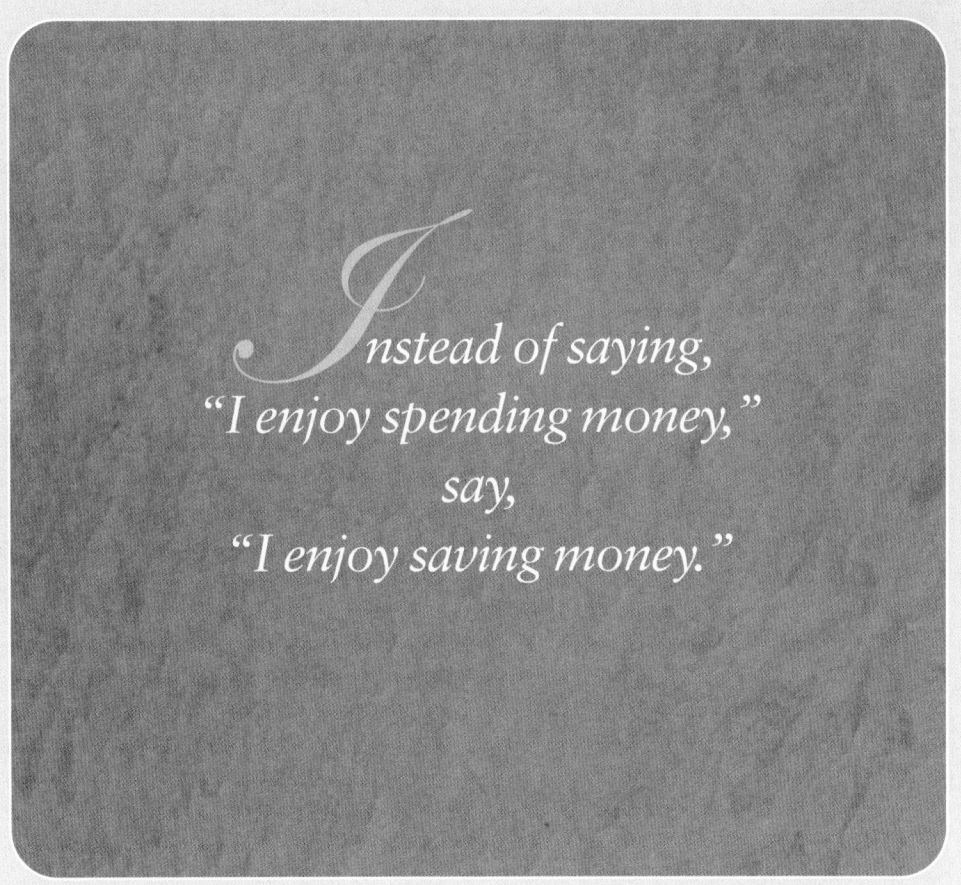

*Instead of saying,
"I enjoy spending money,"
say,
"I enjoy saving money."*

harmony with your dominant thoughts," your financial freedom account begins to grow with the miracle of compound interest.

The more money you have in your bank account, the more energy it generates and more money is attracted into your life. You have heard it said that, "It takes money to make money." This is true. As you begin to save and accumulate money, the universe begins to direct more money towards you to save and accumulate. Everyone who has ever practiced this principle is absolutely astonished at how quickly their financial fortunes change for the better.

The rule for financial independence, once you have rewired your attitude toward money, is to "pay yourself first." Most people save whatever is left over after their monthly expenses, if there is anything left over.

The key however is to pay yourself first,
off the top, any money you earn.

It used to be that, if you saved 10% of your income from your first paycheck until you retired, you would be financially independent, if not rich. Today, financial advisors suggest that you need to save 15% or 20% of your income in order to achieve all your financial goals. Any less than this opens up the risk of running out of money later in life.

When we suggest to people that they need to begin saving 10% of their incomes, they shake their heads. Most people are spending everything they earn today. They have nothing left over. Most people are deeply in debt as well. The idea of saving 10% of their income, off the top, appears impossible. But there is a solution.

Here it is: Begin today to save 1% of your income and learn to live on the other 99%. This is a manageable amount. This is a number that you can get your mind around. It requires only a small amount of self-discipline and delayed gratification for you to save 1% each month. If you are earning $2,000 per month, 1% is $20 per month, or 66 cents per day.

In no time at all, you will become comfortable living on 99% of your income. At that point, you raise your savings level to 2% of your income per month. You adjust your lifestyle to live on 98%. In no time, this will become a habit; you will find it automatic and easy to live on 98% of what you earn.

Month by month, increase your savings level by 1%. By the end of the year, you will probably be saving 10% of your income. Then, something else remarkable will start to happen. Your debts will start to decline. As you become consciously aware of saving your money and moving toward financial independence, you will become more intelligent and thoughtful about each expenditure. You will find yourself spending less and gradually paying off your debts, month by month.

The reward for saving and investing is substantial. Remember we said earlier that, "Happiness is the progressive realization of a worthy ideal." Every time you save a dollar or pay off a dollar of indebtedness, you become happier. You feel more positive and in control of your life. Your brain releases endorphins which give you a feeling of exhilaration and well-being.

Within two years of beginning this process, you will have worked your way out of debt, and begun to accumulate a substantial amount of money in your financial freedom account. As this amount grows larger, you will begin to attract more money and more opportunities to deploy those funds intelligently, so they yield a higher rate of return.

The reward for saving and investing is substantial. Remember we said earlier that, "Happiness is the progressive realization of a worthy ideal." Every time you save a dollar or pay off a dollar of indebtedness, you become happier.

At the same time, your attitude toward money and spending will gradually change. You will become more disciplined and conscientious. You will investigate carefully before you invest. You will study every aspect of a potential business or opportunity. You will be reluctant to part with money that you have worked so hard to accumulate. You will actually begin to reshape your attitude and personality toward money, in a very positive way.

Another helpful discipline to practice is the "WEDGE PRINCIPLE" of financial independence:

As you move forward in life by improving your skills and abilities, your income will increase.
You can use this to your advantage.
It is simple: As your income goes up in the months and years ahead, resolve that you will save 50% of your "increase."

If your income increases by $100 per month, resolve to save $50 per month off the top, and put it into your financial freedom account. Spend the other $50 on your family and improving your lifestyle. **But you must resolve to save *half* of your increase for the rest of your financial life.**

When you pay yourself first by saving 10-15% of your income, and continue saving 50% of your increase for the remainder of your career, you will gain financial independence. You will enjoy financial freedom and join the ranks of the top 5% of people in our society. You will never have to worry about money again.

If you are serious about achieving financial independence, the most important single requirement is self-discipline combined with delayed gratification. Your ability to practice self-mastery, self-control and self-denial throughout your life will not only enable you to achieve all your financial goals, but it will make you successful and happy in everything else you do.

You will never have to worry about money again.

Chapter 6

SELF-DISCIPLINE &

Courage

*"Courage is not the absence of fear;
it is control of fear, mastery of fear."*

MARK TWAIN

Large amounts of self-discipline are needed to deal courageously with all the fear-inducing events of your life. As Churchill said, **"Courage is rightly considered the foremost of the virtues, for upon it, all others depend."**

The fact is that everyone is afraid, and usually of many things. This is normal and natural. Often fear is necessary to preserve life, prevent injury and guard against financial mistakes.

If everyone is afraid, what is the difference between the brave person and the coward? The only difference is that the brave person disciplines himself to confront the fear, to deal with the fear, and to act in spite of the fear.

The coward allows himself to be dominated and controlled by the fear. Someone once said, with regard to warfare that,

"The difference between the hero and the coward is that the hero sticks in there five minutes longer."

Fortunately, all fears are *learned;* no one is born with any fears. Fears can therefore be unlearned, by practicing self-discipline over and over with regard to fear.

The most common fears we experience, which often sabotage all

hope for success, are the fears of failure, poverty and loss of money. These fears cause people to avoid risk of any kind and reject opportunity when it presents itself. They are so afraid of failure that they are almost paralyzed in the face of making decisions.

People also fear the loss of love, the loss of jobs and financial security. People fear embarrassment or being ridiculed. People fear rejection and criticism of any kind. People fear the loss of respect or esteem from others. These and many other fears hold us back throughout life.

The most common reaction to a fearful situation is the attitude of, "I can't!" The inhibitive negative habit pattern, the fear of failure and rejection that holds us back, is experienced physically, starting in the solar plexus. When a person is really afraid, they experience a dry mouth and pounding heart. Sometimes their breathing becomes shallow and their stomach becomes upset.

These are all physical manifestations of the inhibitive negative habit pattern, which we all experience from time to time. Fear paralyzes action. It often shuts down the brain and causes the individual to revert to the fight or flight reaction. Fear is a terrible emotion that undermines our happiness and prevents us from moving forward in life.

Fortunately, because fears are learned, they can be unlearned. We can choose to do the opposite of what fear would normally cause us to do.

Aristotle, in his book, *"The Nichomachean Ethics,"* describes courage as the "Golden Mean." He taught that, "To develop a quality that you lack, act as if you already had that quality in every situation where it is called for." In modern terms we say, "Fake it until you make it."

Psychology states you can actually change your behavior by affirming, visualizing and acting as if you already have the quality you desire. By acknowledging a fear and visualizing a positive outcome, the "I can't" message is replaced with an emphatic, "I can do it!"

Every time you repeat the words,
"I can do it!" with conviction, you cancel or override
your fear and increase your confidence. By repeating this
affirmation over and over, you can eventually
build your courage and confidence to the point
where you are unafraid.

Visualize yourself performing with confidence and competence in an area where you are fearful. Your visual image will eventually be accepted by your subconscious mind as instructions for your performance. Your self-image, the way you see yourself and think about yourself, is eventually altered by feeding your mind these positive mental pictures of yourself performing at your best.

By using the "act as if" method, you walk, talk and carry yourself exactly as you would if you were completely unafraid in a particular situation. You stand up straight, smile, move quickly and confidently, and in every respect pretend as if you already had the courage that you desire.

The Law of Reversibility states that, "If you feel a certain way, you will act in a manner consistent with that feeling." But if you act in a manner consistent with that feeling, even if you don't feel it, the Law of Reversibility will create the feeling that is consistent with your actions. This is one of the greatest breakthroughs in modern psychology.

You develop courage by disciplining yourself to do the thing you fear, over and over, until the fear eventually disappears, which it will.

When I work with companies, they often ask me how to help a salesperson break out of a sales slump. I give them a simple formula that is guaranteed to work every single time. It is called the "100 Call Method." In practicing this method, I instruct the salesperson to go out and call on 100 prospects as fast as he can, without caring whether or not he makes a sale.

When the salesperson doesn't care if he makes a sale, his fear of rejection disappears. He could care less about whether the prospect is interested or not. He has a single focus. It is to make 100 calls as fast as he possibly can.

In 1923, Toastmasters International was formed. Its expressed purpose was to take people who were terrified of public speaking and help them become confident and competent while speaking in front of an audience.

According to the Book of Lists, 54% of adults rate the fear of public speaking ahead of the fear of death. But Toastmasters International had a solution. They created a system of what psychologists call "systematic desensitization."

Once a week, at a luncheon or dinner meeting, small groups of Toastmasters come together. Each person is required to stand up and give a short talk on a specified subject in front of a group of their peers.

At the end of each talk, the speaker receives applause, positive input and comments from the other members. At the end of the evening, each person receives a grade on their talk, even if it was only for thirty or sixty seconds.

After six months of attending Toastmaster's meetings, the individual has publicly spoken twenty-six times, receiving positive applause and feedback each time. His confidence increases dramatically. As a result of those continuous positive experiences, countless Toastmasters have gone on to become excellent public speakers and prominent people in their businesses, organizations and communities.

Your ability to confront your fears, to deal with your fears, and to act in spite of your fears, is the key to happiness and success. One of the best exercises you can practice is to identify a person or situation in your life of which you are fearful, and resolve to deal with that situation immediately. Do not allow it to make you unhappy for another minute. Resolve to confront the situation or person, and put the fear behind you.

The most common quality of leadership is vision. Leaders have a clear vision of where they want to take their organizations. Their personal life also reflects a clear vision of future goals.

*Your ability to
confront your fears,
to deal with your fears,
and to act in spite of your fears,
is the key to happiness
and success.*

The second most common quality of leaders is courage. Leaders have the courage to do whatever is necessary to fulfill the vision.

There are two types of courage you need:

First, you need the courage to launch, to take action, to step out in faith, and to "go boldly where no man has ever gone before."

You need the courage to go "all-in" without any guarantee of success, and with a high possibility of failure. The one failing that holds most people back is that, in spite of all their best intentions, they don't have the courage to take the first step.

The second type of courage you need is called "courageous patience."

This is the ability to hang in there and continue working and fighting after you have done your best before you have seen results.

Many people can force themselves to take action toward a new goal, but when they see no immediate result, they quickly lose heart and revert back to what they've done in the past.

When you identify a fear and discipline yourself to move toward that fear, it decreases and becomes more manageable. As your fears decrease, your confidence grows. Soon, your fears lose their control over you.

When you back away from a fear-inducing situation or person, your fear increases. Soon it preoccupies your thoughts and feelings during the day, and often keeps you awake at night.

The only way to deal with a fear is to address it head-on. **Remind yourself that "denial" is not a river in Egypt.** The natural tendency of many people is to deny that a problem exists. They're afraid to confront it. This is a major source of stress, unhappiness and psychosomatic illness.

Be willing to deal with the situation or person directly. As Shakespeare said, "Take arms against a sea of troubles, and in so doing, end them."

The companion of fear is *worry*. Like twin sisters, fear and worry hang out together. Mark Twain once wrote, "I have worried about a lot of things in life, and most of them never happened."

It has been estimated that 99% of the things you worry about never happen. And most of the things that do happen, happen so quickly that you never have time to worry about them in the first place.

Whenever you worry about something, fill out, "The Disaster Report" on the situation. This destroys fears and worries almost instantly.

*I have worried
about a lot of things in life,
and most of them
have never happened.*

MARK TWAIN

The Disaster Report has four parts:

First, define the worry situation *clearly*.

What exactly is it that you are worried about? Very often, when you take the time to be completely clear about the worry situation, a way to resolve the situation becomes immediately evident.

Second, identify the worst possible thing that could happen if this worry situation were to take place.

Would you lose your job? Would you lose your relationship? Would you lose your money? What is the worst thing that could possibly happen?

Be clear about this. In many cases you will see that, should the worst occur, it will not ruin you. It might be inconvenient or uncomfortable, but you will recover fairly quickly. It's probably not worth all the worry that you are devoting to it.

Third, resolve to accept the worst possible outcome, should it occur.

Say to yourself, "Well, if that happens, it won't kill me. I will find a way to get along."

Most of the stress of worry comes from denial, from not being willing to face the worst possible thing that could happen. But once you resolve in your mind to accept the worst, should it occur, all the worry and stress seems to disappear.

Fourth, begin immediately to improve upon the worst.

Take every step you possibly can to make sure that the worst possible outcome does not occur. Take action immediately. Do something. Get on with it. Act quickly. Get so busy making sure the worst thing does not happen that you have no time to worry.

When you practice the self-discipline of courage, and force yourself to face any fear-inducing situation in your life, your self-esteem goes up, your self-respect improves, and your sense of personal pride grows. You eventually reach the point in life where you are not afraid of anything.

"You gain strength, courage, and confidence by every experience in which you really stop to look fear in the face. You must do the thing which you think you cannot do."

– ELEANOR ROOSEVELT

*In the final analysis,
the only real cure for fear or worry
is disciplined, purposeful action
in the direction of your goals.
Get so busy working on your goals
or the solutions to your problems,
that you have no time to be afraid,
or to worry about anything.*

Chapter 7

SELF-DISCIPLINE &

Responsibility

*"The individual who wants to reach the top in business
must appreciate the might and force of habit.
He must be quick to break those habits that can break him –
and hasten to adopt those practices that will become the habits
that help him achieve the success he desires."*

J. PAUL GETTY

Your ability and willingness to discipline yourself to accept personal responsibility for your life is essential to happiness, health, success, achievement and personal leadership. Accepting responsibility is one of the hardest of all disciplines, but without it, success is impossible.

The failure to accept responsibility and the attempt to foist responsibility onto others has dire consequences. It completely distorts cause and effect, undermines our character, weakens our resolve, and diminishes our humanity.

When I was twenty-one, I was living in a tiny apartment and working as a construction laborer. I had to get up at 5 AM so I could take three buses to work to be there on time. I didn't get home until 7PM, usually exhausted. I was making just enough money to get by, with no car, almost no savings, and just enough clothing for my needs. I had no radio or television. In the evenings, if I had enough energy, I would sit in my small apartment at my little table in my kitchen nook and read.

It was the middle of a cold winter, with the temperature at 35° below Fahrenheit.

One evening, sitting there by myself at the table, it suddenly dawned on me that, "This is my life."

It was like a flashbulb going off in front of my face. I looked at myself and my small apartment, and considered the fact that I had not graduated from high school. The only work I was qualified to do was menial jobs. I earned enough money to pay my basic expenses, but little more. I had very little left over at the end of the month.

It suddenly dawned on me that unless I changed, nothing else was going to change. No one else was going to do it for me. In reality, no one else cared.

I realized at that moment I was completely responsible for my life, and for everything that happened to me, from that day forward. I was responsible.

I could no longer blame my situation on my difficult childhood, or mistakes that I had made in the past. I was in charge. I was in the driver's seat. This was my life, and if I didn't do something to change it, it would go on like this indefinitely, by the simple process of inertia.

This revelation changed my life. I was never the same again. From that moment forward, I accepted more and more responsibility for everything.

I accepted responsibility for doing my job better than before, rather than doing only the minimum to avoid getting fired. I accepted responsibility for my finances, for my health, and especially for my future.

The very next day, I went down to a local book store at lunchtime and began the lifelong practice of purchasing books with information, ideas and lessons that could help me. **I dedicated my life to self-improvement, to continuous learning in every way possible.**

Over time, I learned that 85% of the population never accepts complete responsibility for their lives. They continually complain, criticize, make excuses and blame other people for their unhappiness in life. The consequences of this way of thinking however, can be disastrous. They can sabotage all hopes for success and happiness later in life.

When you are growing up, you become conditioned from an early age, to see yourself as not responsible for your life. This is normal and natural. When you are a child, your parents are in charge. They make all your decisions. They decide what food you will eat, what clothes you will wear, what toys you will play with, what home you will live in, what school you will attend, and what activities you will engage in.

Because you are young, innocent and naive, you do what they want you to do. You have little or no choice or control at all.

As you grow up, you begin to make more of your own decisions in each of these areas. But due to early programming in childhood, you are conditioned unconsciously to feel that someone else is still responsible for your life.

In many cases, we are raised to believe that, if something goes wrong, someone else is responsible. Someone else is to blame. This way of thinking begins in early childhood.

If your parents criticized you or were angry for mistakes you made growing up, you began to automatically assume you were at fault. If your parents punished you physically or emotionally for doing or not doing something that pleased or displeased them, you felt controlled by them, and not responsible for your actions.

If your parents withheld their love by punishing you for not doing something they demanded, you might have grown up with deep feelings of guilt, inferiority, unworthiness and undeservingness. All these negative feelings can prompt you to feel unresponsible for yourself and your life when you become an adult.

The most common feeling we have as adults, if we have been raised

*In many cases,
we are raised to believe that,
if something goes wrong,
someone else is responsible.
Someone else is to blame.
This way of thinking begins
in early childhood.*

in a negative home environment, is the feeling that "I'm not good enough." As a result of this feeling, we compare ourselves unfavorably to others. We think that other people who seem to be happier or more confident are better than us. If they are "worth more" than we are, we must be "worth less." This feeling of inadequacy or worthlessness lays at the root of most personality problems and most political or social problems in our world, both nationally and internationally.

To escape from these feelings of guilt and unworthiness as the result of destructive criticism in childhood, we lash out at our world. If we are unhappy or discontented, our first reaction is to look around and ask, "Who's to blame?"

No one wants to accept responsibility. People spill hot coffee on themselves and in turn sue the fast-food restaurant that sold them the coffee. People get drunk, drive off the road, and then sue the manufacturer of the fifteen year-old car they were driving. People climb up a stepladder, lean over too far and fall. They then sue the ladder manufacturer for their injury. In every case, these people are attempting to escape responsibility for their own behavior by blaming someone else and demanding compensation.

The mark of the leader, the truly superior person, is that he or she accepts complete responsibility for the situation.

It is impossible to imagine a true leader who whines and complains rather than taking action when problems and difficulties occur.

The common denominator of all people is the desire to be happy. In its simplest terms, happiness arises in the absence of negative emotions. Where there are no negative emotions, there are only positive emotions. **Therefore, the elimination of negative emotions is the great business of life – if you truly wish to be happy.**

There are dozens of negative emotions. The most common are guilt, resentment, envy, jealousy, fear and hostility of some kind. **But all the negative emotions ultimately boil down to a feeling of anger, either inwardly or outwardly directed.**

Anger is expressed outwardly when you criticize or attack other people. Anger is expressed inwardly when you bottle it up rather than express it towards others.

Anger is a major source of psychosomatic illness. This happens when "psycho," the mind, makes "soma," the body, sick. Negative emotions expressed in anger, weaken your immune system and make

you susceptible to colds, flu's, and other diseases. Uncontrolled bursts of anger can actually bring about heart attacks, strokes and nervous breakdowns.

Here is the great discovery:

All negative emotions, especially anger,

depend on your ability to blame someone

or something else for something

in your life that you are

unhappy about.

It takes tremendous self-discipline to refrain from blaming others for our problems. It takes tremendous self-discipline to accept complete responsibility for yourself and your actions. It takes tremendous self-discipline to take complete control of your conscious mind and deliberately choose to think positive, constructive thoughts that enhance your life and improve the quality of your relationships and results.

By the Law of Least Resistance, the easiest and most mindless behavior of all is when a person lashes out and blames someone else every time something goes wrong.

The fastest and most dependable way to eliminate negative emotions is to immediately say, "I am responsible!" whenever something happens that triggers anger or a negative reaction of any kind. Quickly neutralize the feelings of negativity by saying, "I am responsible."

It is not possible to accept responsibility and remain angry at the same time. It is impossible to accept responsibility and experience negative emotions. It is impossible to accept responsibility without becoming calm, clear, positive and focused.

As long as you blame someone else for something in your life that you dislike, you remain a "mental child." When you begin to accept responsibility for everything that happens to you, you become a "mental adult."

Many of our biggest problems and concerns in life have to do with money, the earning of it, the spending of it, the investing of it, and especially, the losing of it. Many of our negative emotions are associated with money in some way. But the fact is you are responsible for your financial life. You make the choices and decisions. You are in charge. You cannot blame your financial problems or concerns on other people. You are in the driver's seat.

It is only when you accept responsibility for your income (who chose to accept the job?), your bills (who spent the money?), and your investments (who chose them?), that you move from being an "economic child" to becoming an "economic adult."

There is a direct relationship between the acceptance of responsibility and a feeling of personal control over your life. The more you accept responsibility, the more control you have. There is also a direct relationship between the amount of control you feel you have, and how positive you are. The more you feel you have a high "sense of control" over the important areas of your life, the more positive and happy you will be.

It is not possible to accept responsibility and remain angry at the same time.
It is impossible to accept responsibility and experience negative emotions.
It is impossible to accept responsibility without becoming calm, clear, positive and focused.

Responsibility

In each case, the antidote for negative emotions is to say, "I am responsible," and then look into the situation to find the reason why you are responsible for what happened.

Your intelligence is like a two-edged sword; it can cut in either direction. You can use your intelligence to rationalize, justify and blame other people for things you are unhappy about, or you can use your intelligence to find reasons why you're responsible for what happened.

Even if an accident has occurred, such as your car being hit in the parking lot at work, you may not be a fault for the accident, however you are responsible for your responses, for how you behave as a result.

This sense of "response-ability" is the mark of an excellent person. You take responsibility for your life by resolving, in advance, that you will not become upset or angry over something you cannot affect or change. Just as it is useless to become angry about the weather, it is useless to become angry over circumstances and situations over which you have no control. Do not allow yourself to be angry and unhappy about unhappy experiences or situations from the past. **You say, "What cannot be cured, must be endured."**

All self-discipline, self-mastery and self-control begins with taking responsibility for your emotions. You take charge of your emotions by accepting 100% responsibility for yourself, and for everything that happens to you. **You refuse to make excuses, complain, criticize or blame other people for anything. Instead, you say, "I am responsible" and then get busy resolving the situation in some way.**

When you practice self-discipline and willpower in the acceptance of responsibility, you take complete control of your thoughts and feelings, and become a more effective, happy and positive person in everything you do.

Final Thoughts

It is my hope that this book will help you to truly understand that there are many keys to success, but without self-discipline, none of them work. Is it easy to attain? Of course not. But nothing worthwhile ever is. We must never forget, however, that **the difference in success and failure is not chance, but choice.** And to develop self-discipline we must choose to do what we should do, when we should do it, whether we feel like it or not. To put it another way, **we either choose to manage our life, or...we let our life manage us.**

Here's the good news! **With every tough choice that we make, the next one becomes easier.** Also, with each tough choice we make, our self-respect and self-image is enhanced. And before we know it, choices that were difficult to make in the beginning become our habits. **And when you begin to change your habits, you have truly started down the path to changing your life.**

Here's wishing you...

All the Best,

Brian Tracy

ABOUT THE AUTHOR

Brian Tracy

 Brian Tracy is a professional speaker, trainer, and consultant and is the chairman of Brian Tracy International, a training and consulting company based in Solana Beach, California. He has been a highly successful entrepreneur and in 1981, began teaching his success principles in talks and seminars around the country. Today, his books, audio programs, and video seminars have been translated into thirty-five languages and are used in fifty-two countries.

Tracy has shared his ideas with more than 4 million people in forty-five countries since he began speaking professionally. He has served as a consultant and trainer for more than 1,000 corporations. He has lived and practiced every principle in this book, and has taken himself and countless thousands of other people from frustration and underachievement to prosperity and success.

Brian calls himself an "eclectic reader". He considers himself not an academic researcher but a synthesizer of information. Each year he spends hundreds of hours reading a wide variety of newspapers, magazines, books, and other materials. In addition, he listens to many hours of audio programs, attends countless seminars, and watches numerous videotapes on subjects of interest to him. He is the bestselling author of more than forty books, including Maximum Achievement, Advanced Selling Strategies, Focal Point, and The 100 Absolutely Unbreakable Laws of Business Success. He has written and produced more than 300 audio and video learning programs that are used worldwide.

Brian is happily married and has four children, and lives in San Diego, California. He travels and speaks more than 100 times each year and has business operations in seventeen countries. He is considered to be one of the foremost authorities on success and achievement in the world.

For more information on Brian Tracy, you can visit www.briantracy.com or call (858) 481-2977. Or, you can write to Brian Tracy International at 462 Stevens Ave., Suite 202, Solana Beach, California 92075.

THS DIFFERENCE

If you have enjoyed this book we invite you to check out our entire collection of gift books, with free inspirational movies, at www.simpletruths.com.

You'll discover it's a great way to inspire *friends* and *family*, or to thank your best *customers* and *employees*.

For more information, please visit us at:

www.simpletruths.com

Or call us toll free…

800-900-3427